Daddy, I'm the only woman who thinks of you

How My Daddyless Thoughts turned into my Determination

Carlisa Johnson

Daddy, I'm the only Woman who thinks of you: *How My Daddyless Thoughts turned into my Determination*

Copyright © 2017 Carlisa Johnson

All rights reserved.

ISBN-10: 0692862366
ISBN-13: 978-0692862360

DEDICATION

This book is dictated to my Daughters Mariya and Makayla. As your mother, I learned to grasp life in the best way possible. Your lives may have begun the same as mine, but they will not continue as mine once did. I will continue to teach, nurture, and guide you daily to end the curse of fatherlessness and potential lack in any other area of your lives. You are the offspring of strong, heroic queens and you too are queens. You are royal and intelligent in every way. The absence of your father may have ignited a detrimental cycle in my life as well as my mother's life, but the cycle ends today! You will be different, your daughters will be different, and your granddaughters will be different. Today, I break the curse of fatherlessness.

Mariya and Makayla, you were my "father" (motivation) in life. You taught me how to be tough, responsible, determined, energetic, full of life and most of all how to survive. When you think of your father, you will not have thoughts of sadness, self-blame, insecurity, or hatred. You will love people wisely and accept nothing but the very best God has for you in direct compliment of your purpose. I will forever love and aim to provide you with the *father* things you desire or lack. You will not live as a fatherless daughter.

Love always,
Your Mom

CONTENTS

INTRODUCTION   3

ONE: THE EARLY YEARS:
HOW MY FATHER SET AN UNHEALTHY EXAMPLE   7

TWO: DADDY MADE ME, BUT
MAMA RAISED ME:
HOW MY SINGLE MOTHER HELPED SHAPE MY LIFE   19

THREE : THE OTHER WOMEN:
MY FIRST LOVE AND MY FIRST HEARTBREAK   31

FOUR: THE DADDYLESS BEHAVIOR:
I SEARCHED FOR HIM IN ALL THE WRONG PLACES   41

FIVE: THE DADDYLESS CYCLE:
RAISING TWO FATHERLESS DAUGHTERS   53

SIX : THE DADDYLESS REVELATION:
MY THOUGHTS REVEALED WHO I TRULY WAS   65

Carlisa Johnson

INTRODUCTION

"Fatherlessness didn't strike me as an event.

It was a state of life." –Tom Stoppard

This book illustrates the story of how I constantly thought of my father from childhood to adulthood. I consistently thought of my desire for his presence. Unfortunately for me, father's thoughts remained geared toward other women without the realization I was the one woman thinking of him the most. When I decided to write this book the decision came at the initiation of the adult stage of my life. During this time I thought of my father relentlessly. I pondered each day; "why do I think of this guy so much and why is he on my mind more than anyone else on earth?" When lonely, I thought of my father, when sad, I thought of my father, when hurt, I thought of my father, when I achieved something in life, I thought of my father, and when I look at my children, today I think of my father. Some may ask "why?" Well this intimate look into my life will show you exactly why my Father (Daddy as I would call him) was constantly on my mind. You will also learn how his absence affected many areas of my life.

One day I realized the time had come for my heart and soul to heal. The only way I knew to start the healing was to write the story of my life as it happened growing up without my father.

My sincere desire and ultimate goal for this message is to touch the hearts of fathers and daughters across the world. I want the reader: daughters, a father of a daughter, or men who are planning to become a father, to understand how imperative this next statement is; being in a woman's life from childhood until adulthood can result in a blessing or a curse. In an instant my own life became a curse. Not only did I grow up with a part-time father to no father at all, today my children are living without their father as well. There are so many daughters living today with struggles that are a direct result of a father's absence.

Think for a moment.

How many daughters can honestly say they think of their father as much as their father's wife, girlfriend, or mistress thinks of him?

Daughters, this book is for you. As daughters our constant wonder is if it is our fault our father was absent. Please know that thinking of your father is not crazy nor is it foolish. If any of you were like me, you had your father in your life, he pulled away from your life, then you experienced your very first real heartbreak and you will always remember that heartbreak.

I know many women share my story, but so many are too hurt

tell their own or try to find ways to avoid thoughts of their relationship with their father. Many choose to steer away from things that would include a fathers presence or input and choose to delay overcoming struggles of being a fatherless daughter.

Fathers, this book is especially for you. Men, you are our heroes, protectors, and earthly providers. We daughters don't receive protection and provision and feel our lives are overlooked when you choose other women and commit your interests to things and people outside of us. Fathers, I want you to know that no matter where you go in life, if you have a daughter please know she will always remain the number one woman who thinks of you no matter what. She needs you more than you know.

This book is a mission for my healing and for all daughters and daughters to come to healing across the world. This story will show how my father's absence became my motivation. I may have been thinking of him constantly, but that constant thinking became my determination.

I was a fatherless child who maneuvered life by doing fatherless things, but during this journey my father was still on my mind. I was put in a difficult place. It was hard for me to determine what a man should look like or how a man should be; more importantly it clouded my view of what love was.

ONE

THE EARLY YEARS

Parents often overlook and underestimate their example. Whatever they do around us and whatever they teach us will be the example we identify with for the rest of our lives. What I experienced from my father's absence would affect me for days to come. I didn't realize this in the beginning. My example from *daddy* is a little different from most, yet similar to a lot of women. The one thing I can remember from childhood is being with my father. Whenever my father came around, the first thing he and I would do is play and tussle. At times like these I could be me, my age and myself. To me, that was love. My mom worked so much that showing love toward me was not priority, at least that is what I gathered. Either that or she simply lacked the tools to give me what I needed from her. Nonetheless, I knew I could get the love I warranted from my father. I always heard stories of how my great grandmother adored me, but I can only remember the love and affection my father showed me as a child. You see, as a young girl I believed I was the epitome of a "daddy's girl," yet was I really? I've questioned this notion every day of my life. Was I really his baby girl? Growing up I didn't know if I were acting as a child or an adult when it came to the love and affection I so longed for from my parents, especially my father. I felt I were my father's "main squeeze" because I was the only girl who believed I needed his love and affection. Now, you may ask, "is she talking about molestation from her father?" No, of course not. Unfortunately, molestation came from someone I believed to be my father, but I will unravel those details further within a future chapter. I'm simply stating I wanted no one's love and affection the way I desired my fathers because I wanted to remain a "daddy's girl." Though it may have been what I aimed for, my father was not overly affectionate, yet had his ways of showing his love for me.

During those times we didn't know what a love language was, but my mom showed hers through working hard and providing things for me whereas my father showed his love through a playful spirit and aggression. The "pick me up daddy", the "stop tickling me til' I laughed the pee out of me" daddy was my favorite. Yes, those were the memories I still meditate on until this very day. I think of my father so much because those memories didn't last long. Moments like this faded when daddy found another "main squeeze"—another woman.

I always wonder what happened with my parent's relationship. They quarreled so much their relationship became a blur throughout all the dysfunction they created. I always blamed my dad for leaving my mother, but now I question if he really left her. Was it all his fault? He didn't realize it was me who was lost and needed refuge as a child. It was me. I needed his love and affection, and I would live the rest of my life doing fatherless things because he chose another woman.

As weekends came and went, time with my father began to fade away weekend after weekend. My mother would always say, "your daddy is probably with that woman" or, "he's probably at the club dancing." The sound of a huge rust red and white truck (the truck my father faithfully drove until this very day) coming up a hill alerted me that my dad was there to get me! As a little girl, I would always look forward to the weekend because I knew I would see my father. My mom always called my father a "weekend dad." I never did understand why in the beginning, but the older I became, the more I understood. I would always notice all of my cousins with their dad every day of the week and wonder why my dad wasn't as present, but I got used to the weekends. I accepted it as okay, but it wasn't. A girl can learn to nurture from her mother, but a girl needs her father to be her hero. Even when my parents were together my dad was still a weekend dad and lived with his parents. Sometimes I wonder if by my dad living with his parents was a reason he wasn't able to be a father to me, yet and still he had time to be with other women. I really didn't know much about my father's relationship with his parents, but I knew his actions toward me had a lot to do with how he was raised. My father didn't know what needing his quality time and presence meant to me, therefore he gave the minimum just to say he was being a father. The behavior of my father was somewhat weird because he was a very shy man even when it came to me and I was his daughter! I never knew where all the shame came from, but I just smiled a lot as he did and later in life became and very shy person as well. You see I was learning to be just like my dad without realizing much of what I picked up were not good traits to learn.

Considering my dad was a "weekend dad", there were a lot of

moments I felt abandoned when he would drop me off and leave. I was extremely happy when he would come back to pick me up again. Imagine the emotional ups and downs I faced as a child from the back and forth visits. I wondered why I didn't get the 24/7 time or the live-in dad as others around me. I can recall acting out badly during the week just to hear my mom say, "I'm going to send you with your daddy." I did this quite a lot. On the inside I thought, "good, I want to go be with him anyway, but all of this was a figment of my imagination. In reality, my mom would have never done that because she had her own emotional issues toward my father. During the time I spent with my father on the weekend, my dad still lived with his parents and I never knew why. You see, my time with my father was much like a date. He would pick me up and as we traveled to his house in the country, he would play music and sing to me the whole trip. My father sang to me every time he picked me up and until this day I hear my father singing in my head. Of course, I was always shy and blushed the entire trip, but guess what…I became attracted to people who would sing to me without knowing if they really loved me. Sometimes during our trips, we would stop to get snacks along the way or wait until we got to his house because we knew my grandmother (my father's mother) had already cooked or had sweets all around.

During the time spent at my grandmother's house my father didn't spend much time with me because he was either attending his horses, repairing a car, getting ready for the night out, or asleep. Though our time was often compromised by other things, as long as my dad picked me up and had me with him, I concluded that was enough for me, but was it really? At that age, I didn't realize that this weekend process with my father was setting me up for a world of future destruction.

Many fathers don't grasp that when it comes to time, the lack of it spent with your daughter will affect her for the rest of her life. My dad gave me part-time love and time and as I got older I thought that was the best love because my father *was* my best love. As I got older I would settle for part-time love and time spent with others throughout the rest of my life. This is the example that shaped my thoughts of my father as I grew older. Life will send many examples your way, but I'm an observer when it comes to learning. I observed my father's ins and outs and made his character my own. In spite of our various imbalances, I admired my father because growing up, I felt he would be my king, my protector and my hero for the rest of my life.

The example my dad showed wasn't the best, but it was the best for me because I thought maybe that's how it should be--boy was I soon awakened. I watched my father do everything for the short period he was around. He was a very creative and crafty man with a lot of DETERMINATION. You may ask why I chose to put this word in all caps. You will understand later on as you uncover how thoughts of my father shaped my life.

My time with my father was precious to me, but I don't think it was that deep for him. Many fathers believe that as long as they put in the time that's all a girl needs, but it's not the time, it's what you do with the time. My father didn't realize that during these times I was falling in love with him and using our dysfunctional relationship as an example of love for the rest of my life. My daddy was my first connection and most important man in my life, but get this, I have no pictures of my father and I together. No photos of him holding me or me sitting in his lap, so why do I constantly think of him?

I gather the connection wasn't physical. The connection of my father was blood that resides in me from being emotionally connected to him no matter what. I feel that connection I had with my daddy was one of a kind. It was a connection he would never feel or get from any other woman. He didn't realize that the connection he had with his daughter was a connection that will never leave no matter how many women came into his life. Now, some may say since I was a daddy less daughter how do I know what it means to be a good or bad father? I'm not saying I know what it means, but I do know that my soul needed my father, my heart needed my father, and mind needed my father. The vivid images of my daddy I received on the weekend gave me some idea of what my father should have been. Seeing others grow up around me with their fathers present full-time showed me what my father should have been doing. There were times I compared my daddy to other fathers which brought confusion and thoughts of "I wish." I wish my father was with me every day, I wish my father would take me here, I wish my father was like him, and so on. Those thoughts would cause me to overthink constantly. My daddy wasn't at every function and every event of my life, but I would always see him at the basketball and football games at my school and not to mention the club every time it opened. Imagine seeing your ex at a function, not seeing them for days, weeks, or months and you get this feeling inside like "oh he or she can be there, but can't come and see me" yeah that's how my thoughts were when I saw my father at events. See this was the beginning of seeking attention, my insecurities, my overthinking, my heartache, and my emptiness.

Dear Daddy,

I miss you and I don't think I can wait until this weekend. Can you come often, like during the week. I know you and mommy are fussing, but make it right and come home, though I know this isn't home for you. I sleep with momma because I'm scared, so when you get here I know I can sleep by myself because you will get the boogie man for me and mommy. Daddy, I hope to see you soon!

Your baby girl

I was too little to remember when I wrote this one, but I will never forget how I long for my daddy to be home with us. This example of my father became the backbone of my life and I began to accept his inconsistent presence in my life not knowing it wasn't enough to guide me for the rest of my life. Hey, it was good enough for me as a child because I identified with what was shown to me. If my father showed me coming around sometimes was good then I thought it was the best. If my daddy showed me spending time with me on the weekend was enough for him, it was enough me. As I mentioned, this was the example I observed and as children we believe our parents give us the best. In my mind, the best was whatever my daddy gave and showed me, but I was fooled. His example haunted me throughout my life and gave me thoughts like no other. I used this example throughout my life because I had the image of my daddy in my head, the type of love he showed me, and the example of my daddy. This marked the initiation of my searching for him in all the wrong people and places. I struggled throughout school and felt it was because of need of attention and love. As I mentioned, in the beginning mom worked a lot and daddy was part-time so when I went to school I demanded attention through bad behavior. At times I didn't know I was using it as an excuse, but those thoughts of my daddy made me feel I could go to school and act out if I wanted to. I didn't realize that the thoughts I had as a child were already starting to shape my life. Seeing the example of someone can be good or bad and it's up to us how we will use the example when it is placed upon us.

When the example is coming from the most important person in your life, for me my father, you take the good and the bad you see. Remember your father is your earthly protector so technically bad wasn't a part of my thoughts. It was all good when it came to my daddy. My mother would tell me quite a bit that I looked and acted just like my daddy and I would actually feel good inside instead of bad. I know that may seem strange, but my daddy was my all and knowing I had anything that was a part of him was a blessing to me. God, I loved that man!

Now, your example of your father may be different from

mine, but in my daddyless mind my example was just how I saw it and how things were dealt to me. It was perfect for me, at least I thought. What I didn't know was that the example of my father would create a mind of dark, lonely, and painful days ahead. I didn't know that the revolving doors of my father's life would bring abandonment issues. I had no idea that my place in his priorities would ignite the trend of me putting my own self last.

Every time my daddy left I wondered when he would come back. This ignited thoughts such as, "I'm not good enough" or "everyone always leaves me." These thoughts plagued me in relationships throughout life. Oh yes, I didn't realize all of this! During the onset of this way of thinking, I was too young to think of my future, but my daddy was old enough to know that the example he set would affect me for days to come. Maybe my father didn't notice this. It could also be possible he just didn't care. In the present day I still don't know the answer. As I matured and after so many years of believing my dad's example was the best thing for my life, I realized his example was actually ruining my life.

We as women tend to set forth the realization that our fathers are the ones who will dictate how we view men, trust people, how we love, and how we raise our own children. I thought of this example far too long. I was ready to change my thinking and structure my own example; not only for me, but for my daughters. The struggle was very real. Don't get me wrong, I benefitted from many of the right things a woman needed to see growing up, but my dad on the other hand showed me how to give up, walk away, not care, and how to be selfish. The worst part about all of this is my dad didn't know he was teaching me these things. I'm just telling you that his example was probably perfect to him as well.

Many fathers don't realize that in order to be a good example you have to know the example you are showing. You can't be a good example with no rhyme or reason to your example.

"A person cannot give you what they don't have or don't know themselves"

I realize my father just didn't have the example he needed to give me, but I still thought of his example every day of my life and craved it. My daddy may not have possessed the tools necessary to be the ultimate example, however that excuse was not enough for me to cease thoughts of why he didn't stay, why he didn't keep our family together, and why he didn't love the only woman he helped create--me. Those questions linger in my head with each passing day.

For this man to constantly linger in my thoughts he had to be some type of father figure to me, but the relationship was DYSFUCTIONAL. When I think of dysfunction I think of something that just isn't right. Every time I thought of my daddy, a dysfunctional example would pop up in my head and that's where my determination came from; not allowing the example of my father to destroy me. I didn't want to live dysfunctional, but I still loved and wanted my daddy. I wanted to be normal, not dysfunctional or bad, but in my school days badness was all I knew to be to get what I wanted. I learned I had to be my own example through my experiences and trials in life. The example of my daddy motivated me to push and be all I could be.

Dear Daddy:

I really want you to be with mama. It's getting hard around here. Mama is stressed, working as hard as she can, but I need you here with us. I don't like the man mama is with, so can you come and just make it right with mama? Everybody has their daddy around accept for me and it makes me feel bad a lot. I know you are out there with other women, but mama and I need you more than them. I need you daddy. You know I'll be a woman soon and this probably won't even matter anymore.

Your baby girl

Guess what? It mattered a great deal. When I became a woman things got worse with my life. Lord knows I needed this man I called *daddy*. I cried many nights to see the example of him more often, but I didn't. My daddy was a need not a want and fathers around the world must know this. You are a need to your daughters. The women you chase or crave to be with are just a want that can be fulfilled anyway, but the presence of a father cannot be fulfilled by just anyone. There is no replacement and no substitutes. A father has to be the person who helped create you.

Carlisa Johnson

TWO

DADDY MADE ME, BUT MAMA RAISED ME

Ok so by now you're familiar with the example given to me by my daddy. It wasn't a pretty one. The fact it added on to the shaping of my life wasn't pretty either. I'm using the example of two people; my father as a weekend Dad and my mom as a single parent., so imagine my striving to figure life out throughout my childhood journey. Usually you are under one teaching and one roof with two parents, but rearing was totally different. My mom was a single mom and a work -a-holic who thought that by over working and providing things there would be sufficiency for all of my and my brother's needs. Of course it was not.

When I was born, I was swamped around a lot of adults. Because of this I started thinking like an adult at an early age. Mom was raised by her grandmother so I wasn't around my cousins much. I was basically the only child before my brother came along, so I had to grow up at an early age. More often than not, as children we are shaped by the person who feeds us. Well, mom did just that. She never let me and my brother go hungry or miss a meal. I watched my mom day after day, but I still missed my father being there. My mother alone just wasn't enough. Now I'm not saying my mom wasn't my everything because she is, but I needed more than the nurturing presence of my mother in my life. My mother couldn't give me an example of how to stay away from men who loved you more on your outside than the inside. My mother couldn't tell me what men think when it comes to choosing a woman. Most of all, my mother couldn't tell me how a man should love you. I needed my father for those things.

My mother found herself dealing with her own issues with finding love after she and my father's relationship ended. She would always tell me how she was raised. She stated her father took her away one day after he and her mother were arguing and she lived with her grandmother ever since. I never understood the story of her childhood because she didn't talk about it much. No doubt I always wondered why grandmother never returned her to her parents, but the question was never answered. Basically, I believe my mother lacked the wherewithal when it came to showing me love, affection and attention because she likely never received it herself.

As a child I was unaware of this, but as an adult I can feel the full brunt of what I lacked from my parents as a child.

I had to find it on my own.

While my mother carried on as a workaholic, trying to find love at an early age was work as well. My mom's paternal uncles and aunts were like siblings because she was raised along with them after her father took her. After learning this, imagine how my relationships with people were progressing. I was being spoiled by my great-grandmother, and uncles and aunts, but there was still a lot missing. Those relationships with them were temporary. Many of them moved up north and I had to create new bonds here and there with family members. Keep in mind this was the start of consistent "temporary relationships" throughout life. I thought this was normal, but it really wasn't. While trying to raise me, my mother strived to keep herself together as well. When I matured, I realized she really didn't have the best of life either. I really don't remember my father being around much while we were living with my maternal family, but in order for me to exist he had to have shown up at some point in time.

"The most important thing a father can give his children is to love their mother."

After my mom and dad's on and off relationship ended, life became confusing and questionable. I remember my mom picking up everything and leaving the South to move to Cleveland, OH. Oh boy, this was not the place for me! I was so sad and angry. I complained daily. I was bullied at my new school and we lived with my aunt who was really strict on things. I yelled all the time, "I want my daddy!" As a result of all of this; my mom not finding work and the unhappiness of my brother and I, she decided to move back to the South. Once again, temporary relationships would become a normal thing for me.

My mom continued to work hard, but also continued searching for love for herself. Imagine us both searching for love at the same time. I realize my mom was trying to fill the void of being raised differently than her siblings. My father had left and she simply wanted love. Flash forward, I began doing the same with my daughters present. I searched for love and tried to fill voids of my past. I didn't realize it, but I had the love I desired for quite some time. We will talk about the relationships I have with my daughters in a later chapter.

My mother thought a stepfather would help her with me and my brother. This plan may have worked, but I would have never received a stepfather as my father. I wanted my biological father more than any stepfather, good or bad, but most stepfathers weren't a good example for me. By the time my mom began having other relationships, the anger over my father's absence had already developed.

I didn't get along with any of my stepfathers, but my mom tried her best to make me. My mom missed the fact I was lacking the love, attention, and affection I needed from her and my dad. She was so overworked, she didn't notice how my life began to form in a bad way. Alcoholism was a trait of my mom's side of the family; mostly with the men. Whenever my mom got a new boyfriend, he would be an alcoholic too. Until this day I cannot stand an overly drunk person. It's a turnoff for me. My father's side of the family didn't drink at all, so I guess I inherited that from him. Don't get me wrong. I drink occasionally, but seeing another person drunk, particularly one I am dating, is so not good--maybe because I grew up around far too much of this. See, when my mother moved back to the south, my uncle, who was much like a brother to my mom, started looking after me and my brother while my mom worked. My uncle was a man who loved to cook, eat, and drink. He worked himself until his poor health wouldn't let him anymore. He had a history of being overweight. During those times, he ran a shot house. Men, women, crackheads, and drunks were in and out of my uncles shot house. I learned how to cook and a clean during these years because often times my uncle would be too drunk and tired to look after me. Lord knows I saw so much growing up in that house. I always stayed in the back living room area and watched cartoons, but sometimes men would look back into the room and try to flirt with me and such. Yes, at an early age I was experiencing all of this. I fully developed physically at a young age, so the drunks didn't care if I was a child or not. Thank God no one ever did me harm at my uncle's house, however harm did come when my mother met another guy whom I will refer to as stepfather number one.

By the time my mother met stepfather number one, I was getting used to being without my father as well as his occasional absence. This first stepfather was something different. He was older, charming, and giving. I really thought he would be the one to make my mom happy and help her provide for us so my mom wouldn't have to work so hard, however that wasn't the case. Instead he was a man who came to take from me as well. Many details of my story were very ordinary happenings for those in the south and often their response to such was "just pray about it."

In my life I needed more than just prayer.

What stepfather number one took from me was more than ordinary. It was life changing for me in a major way. Me, my mom, and brother we were both persuaded by this first stepfather because he had a nice house, car, a lot of land (which is a plus in the south), and money. I really thought I was going to get anything I wanted and he was going to replace the missing void of my father.

I was fooled.

While my mother worked diligently, stepfather number one was now looking after me and my brother. My brother was a toddler at the time and fell in love with him. He always wanted to go over to his house and I had to go everywhere my brother went. My mom had begun an over-night job and we would stay overnight at stepfather number one's house. I remember it as if it occurred yesterday.

One night he fed my brother and me a big meal and let us watch TV for the rest of the night. I thought I was in heaven. My brother and I were in the other bedroom. Considering we were full of food and TV, my brother would fall asleep instantly. After a short while I would too, but on this night stepfather number one came to check on us as he always did and found my brother asleep. He woke me and said, "come into the room with me", half asleep and half-alert, I just went. I thought I was just going to go back to sleep, but I was wrong. He laid me on his bed, turned the TV on and lied down next to me. Keep in mind I believed this was fine because whenever I spent the night at my dad's house we would sleep with him and nothing ever happened to us, however this night stepfather number one took my innocence away from me.

After lying down beside me he began touching and rubbing my body and asked me to do the same to him. I was very afraid and didn't know what was going on. He decided to climb on top of me and whispered into my ear, "you better not tell nobody." I did just that, I didn't tell anyone because I was too afraid. This sexual abuse from stepfather number one went on for months until my mom left after discovering how crazy he was. I kept secret what he did to me until I was 30 years old; that was 20 years ago.

The residue of the molestation I suffered damaged my trust and security towards people. In those days I was taught to keep quiet about those type of things. I did exactly that when stepfather number one took my innocence. The sexual abuse I endured left many scars of guilt, anger, and fear. The scars made my fatherless wounds even deeper. I knew one day I would have to overcome it all and tell someone though I carried the burden for years. I went on with my life trying to blind it away as if the abuse never happened, but my promiscuous behaviors reminded me of it. For some reason, I believed if I told anyone I would be harmed by him again, get blamed for it, or no one would believe me.

Stepfather number one came around as a family friend after he and my mother separated. I can remember when I became pregnant with my first child. With a grin on his face, he asked, "what are you doing having a baby?"

I could have punched him in the face.

I blamed him for much of my sexual behavior as well. I wondered how he could ask me something like that knowing what he'd done to me. I believe the sexual abuse of my childhood initiated depression, insomnia, and anxiety in my life. My sexual dysfunction was a part of the map of my life and it was leading me down plenty of danger roads I will discuss further in the next chapters. When I became an adult I knew it was time to tell my mother about what happened to me, but I was very afraid. I can remember the day I decided to see a counselor just to receive advisement as to how I should approach the subject. She stated the first thing I needed to do was tell my mother and family. I was very hesitant, but I knew it was a must. One day, I mustered up the courage to talk with my mother. It took me forever to come out and say it. My mother kept asking, "What is it Carlisa?" I immediately broke down into tears and told her I was molested by stepfather number one. My mother was in disbelief. She wanted to know why I didn't tell her when it happened. I told her not only was I afraid at the time of the incident, I actually thought it was acceptable that it happened to me. My mother's reaction wasn't major like I expected. She stated "well there's nothing we can really do now because you waited so late to say something." I wasn't sure how I was supposed to take that response, but I took it. Telling her what happened to me was a heavy burden lifted off my chest. I instantly felt the relief. After my mom learned this secret, it was then time to tell my father. At the time, I was still trying to establish a relationship with him, so when I would go back home to visit I would try to see him. My father's reaction was actually the reaction I would have wanted to see from my mom. I was shocked when he stated, "I'm going to say something to him!" I immediately told my dad, "no", because I didn't want to cause anymore drama. I was surprised at my dad's reaction, but also happy because that is the type of reaction and protection I needed from him as a child. I felt that if I had this part of him back then, maybe this would have never happened.

Another burden was lifted.

I realized if I continued to keep my molestation a secret, I would still be bound. Telling someone was a channel to receive help and freedom from the behaviors and emotions molestation caused. I wish I would have told my family earlier in life at the time of this incident. If I would have done that, maybe I would be telling a different story with a brighter side.

That secret tore my life apart and added another layer of anger, hurt, and sadness to my life toward my parents, especially my dad. After the molestation I daily declared; " if my dad had been in my life it would have never happened." I needed his protection while my mother tried to raise me.

As a child, its never your fault when someone violates your body even if you continue to allow them to persuade you. Molestation is a crime no matter how the predator portrays it. TELL SOMEONE and be FREE!

"I cannot think of any need in childhood as strong as the need for a father's protection."

- Sigmund Freud

I was still dealing with the "weekend father", the hurt, pain, and secret of stepfather number one, and the searching to fill the voids of my life. Imagine a child walking around daily holding all of this inside, but too young to realize how it would affect her in the journey of life.

Stepfather number two came. By the time of his arrival, I was fed up and didn't get along with him at all. My mom would always say "Carlisa, you ought not act like that, God is going to punish you," but she really didn't know what I was feeling and holding inside. I didn't want to deal with another stepfather. Once again, I just wanted my Daddy. After the downfall of stepfather number two due to fighting and alcoholism, I believe my mom was fed up as well, yet continued working and providing for us. Still, we were all empty. We were all full of hurt and pain baring a surplus of voids. My mom continued to keep me in church and school and my brother was getting older. He began to realize what was going on, but didn't really express it that much. Until this day me and my brother's relationship is not the best and I really don't understand why. It could be due to the fact every relationship we have had since childhood has not been the best, therefore we never developed a good one.

Stepfather number three was introduced to my life and he was the last, thank God! Stepfather number three wasn't perfect, but he tried. He couldn't give me what he didn't have. He came from a very large family of 13 siblings who lived in a very poor town in the South. He was jobless and an extreme alcoholic. Initially, he made my mom happy for the most part, but by that point in my life, I really didn't care anymore of what he could offer me and my brother. I was just going along with the "show" again.

I had become a teenager and a very promiscuous one, or as true southerners would say, I had become "fast." After I was robbed of my innocence, I assumed the molestation played a major part in my promiscuity. Again my mom was still beyond occupied with work and now stepfather number three was looking after us. He would always take us to his family house which was in another city (about 20 miles away) and for the most part it was fun, but could have been better. The boys of the family would always try to come onto me desiring I have sex with them. Being the promiscuous girl I was, I participated.

I will never forget the one night when three guys (stepfather number three's nephews) ran a "train" on me. I felt so violated and hurt, but allowed it because I truly believed that was the way a boy or man showed his love for me. Losing my virginity at an early age was a shaping and molding of my womanhood that took years to change. No one had any idea of this and it was yet another secret I lived with. After a while my mom stopped me from going to stepfather number three's family house because she said I was too "fast." By that time, I was talking back to my mom and had taken on a rebellious attitude.

After 13 years of my mom's marriage to stepfather number three he suddenly passed from heart complications that came as a result of his alcoholism. Throughout these years I saw my mom shed so many tears, wear so much hurt, and work far too hard. Yet and still something inside of me was DETERMINDED to never end up as she did because of all that happened to me.

What I learned from my mom was this; even though life throws some unexpected things toward you, you must keep moving. One thing about my mother is that she kept her life moving forward no matter what happened. She may have missed out on a lot with me and my brother but she stayed afloat without drowning in her own pain and misery. I watched her and her actions every day and thought her example was the way to live, but some things I learned from her affected my life in many ways. Sometimes in life a person can only try and that's their personal best.

Throughout the journey of life I blamed my mother for so much and praised my father for doing less. It should have been the opposite. My mom may have been looking for love in all the wrong places, but my father could have been in the right place to show me what love is and what love does. Sometimes I think to myself, "if I had told my dad about the molestation when it happened or about the guys who ran a train on me, would he have come back?" Probably not because the events of my life were in a divine order. Some would ask, "where was your daddy during all of this?" Well the next chapter will tell you. I was still determined to bring my father back into our lives, but he had other agendas.

THREE

THE OTHER WOMEN

"Kids have a hole in their soul in the shape of their dads. If a father is unwilling or unable to fill that hole, it can leave a wound that is not easily healed."

-Roland Warren

The urban dictionary states; a first love is the one you first truly have feelings for: the one person you will never forget. Their love will leave an imprint on your heart that will be there forever. Your first love will be one hardest to get over and the one you will still love even after they have broken you down. I can say this definition is true and correct.

My daddy was my first love and I once thought I was his as well. When I was little my dad never said, "I love you" with his words, but the things he did made me feel he loved me. He wasn't there to support me in every event, but he was the first person who showed me emotional love through his singing. My dad was an awesome singer and every weekend he would pick me up and play several songs to me that made me look into his eyes all shy and stuff. That was a part of the love my daddy showed me. The more he sung to me each weekend, the more I fell in love with the man who helped create me. I will never forget this one particular song my daddy would always sing by Freddie Jackson; one of his favorite

R&B artists during that time. The song was entitled "You Are My Lady." Oh boy! Every time my dad sang that song to me I would smile from the inside out and knew there was no woman on earth who could take my place. At the time my mother and father's relationship was up and down. I'm not certain what all happened and can't speak on it much, but I do know my dad loved music and singing and that was one way he would express his love to me and others. Since childhood I would hear the words of that song and instantly think of my father and our relationship. Some mornings, some nights, some days I would hear that song over and over again. I didn't realize it would haunt me for the extent of my life to date. I believed that no matter how my dad or other men treated me, I was still their lady; I was fooled!

There's something that I want to say
But words sometimes get in the way
I just want to show
My feelings for you
There's nothing that I'd rather do
Than spend every moment with you
I guess you should know
I love you so
You are my lady
You're everything I need and more
You are my lady
You're all I'm living for

Daddy, I'm the only woman who thinks of you

- Freddie Jackson

Those where the words to the song my daddy sang to me every weekend. Imagine your "weekend" daddy singing those words to you only to bring you home, drop you off and disappear again for 4-5 days. Weekends were when the dark feelings began to return. During weekends my heart felt this ache that I just might feel for the rest of my life. A dad is the first love a girl should have but should never be her first heartbreak. My daddy broke my heart way before a man or anyone did. During my childhood, his love made me feel I didn't deserve anything less, but the heartbreak made me feel less than everything throughout my life afterwards. My daddy's love gave me a sense of protection during the moments he was present with me, but when he wasn't around I would always feel afraid. For me, this was nothing less than an emotional roller coaster. I didn't realize that with my dad being my first love, no one would be able to replace his love or fill the hole in my heart after he began to fade from my life more and more.

I can remember when I first felt the pain of jealousy, but at that particular age I didn't know what jealousy was. My dad had moved on and began dating another woman; the true start of my heartbreak. Early in the relationship with my father, he would pick me up on weekends and it was only him and myself before my brother came along. Now, it was the "other woman" and her child tagging along, at least that was what my mother called her. My father never knew I hated having a "stepmother" because I felt she took my father away from my mother and me. My mom told me so many stories of how my father cheated with this woman and how she tore us apart. I believed my mother's story over my fathers. My father would always claim her side of the story wasn't true, however at the time I really didn't care if it wasn't I only wanted my father back into my life.

More often than not, whenever I was with my father and stepmom, we were all over the place. I felt like my dad began to be a father more to her child than his own. My daddy was very handsome and had a very deep love for women. He was a "philandering" man who loved women. I really don't know how many other women there were but one thing I can attest to is that he only had me around one woman consistently throughout my life. After my dad married her I became even more furious about this woman. I really don't know how I discovered my father had gotten married. There was no wedding or anything. Still until this day my father and "stepmom" are married and I have no idea how long they've been married. I guess I really don't care. I felt I was no longer getting the attention and love I needed from my dad and because of that I developed anger that may be with me for the remainder of my life.

The thoughts began to fester more and more and I began to question my dad's love for me. Did he forget his first love? Some may believe I acted as a spoiled child, but keep in mind this was my father and I was already fighting to keep the little time we had on the weekends. This was the start of my determination. Many believed I was a determined woman from the womb, but as far as I can remember my determination started at early age with the attempt to maintain a relationship with my father. Determination is when you keep aiming to fix or do something no matter how it looks, or who or what is involved. After my father got with another woman I was determined to keep our relationship, yet too young at the time to hold it all together. During the time I became bitter and angry. I also felt my father left me for another woman. Many nights I would sing myself to sleep with the many songs my dad would sing to me. This developed my love for music and singing. I was trying to prove to my father that his new woman wouldn't love him like his daughter. I was determined to show him what I was lacking while the other women were gaining.

Quite a few fathers seem unaware of the that, then and now. Though a relationship may fall apart between a child's parents, the child should still experience sufficiency in everything they need. The child should be the main focus beyond the demise of his or her parent's relationship. A father's hurt should not become the child's responsibility. The aforementioned may come across very clean cut, but in reality many children feel the full brunt of a his or her parent's broken relationship and are often left abandoned, held responsible for the lack and hurt, and utterly lost. I heard a preacher once say, "a child doesn't know himself because there was no father present in his life." Fathers are the key source of a child knowing themselves and when the father is not there that child may live their whole life searching for their identity. The lack of my father's presence made me stronger, but I'm still in search of who I am. I had to declare who I was at an early age and until this day I still declare I am somebody regardless of the lack of my father's presence. The heartbreak broke me for years to come, but it broke me into determination. The pieces of the determination were broken into strength, courage, and empowerment. Those pieces kept me together even while searching for my father in people and things. Many have claimed a father teaches a daughter her worth and this is very true for me. The heartbreak that stemmed from my father ignited life's teaching of my worth. I began to feel worthless after my dad faded out of my life. I felt I wasn't worth being his daughter or worth enough for him to stay. As his involvement decreased, I began finding myself. Healing a broken heart from your father's absence is not easy. I will likely live my entire life on this journey to total healing. I tried to fill the void with my stepfathers, but there was nothing they could do or say that would make me forget my father and wish he was there instead of the "stepfathers". Nothing could fill the void of my father, and I wondered everyday if he would come back and be a part of our family again. That question within my heart was beginning to slowly receive an answer.

A Father's Heartbreak

Daddy, you broke my heart after
You left my life in the rain
I see you with her, but I'm the
One that's in pain
Daddy, you were my hero and
I was your lady, but since you left my days

Have been crazy
You created a void in my life only to fill hers
But I'm determined to take
Those broken pieces and prove to you I am Yours

Fathers flaws become an impact not only to their own lives, but to their daughters lives as well. Victoria Scaunda stated, "Most fathers don't see the war within the daughter, her struggles with conflicting images of the idealized and flawed father, nor her temptation both to retreat to Daddy's lap and protection and to push out of his embrace to that of beau and the world beyond home."

My father may have had many flaws that I will likely never know, but I do know he was still perfect for me even after the heartbreak. It's as if I wanted to give him chance after chance to get right, to make it right, or just to be right by my side. I wonder everyday if he knew that the girl who has been broken-hearted by him is the one girl he helped create; me, his daughter. Fathers all over the world may have broken the hearts of many other women, but the one heart that matters most is his daughter's. A woman's heart can be healed after being broken by her partner, but when her heart is broken by her father it takes more time, heartache, pain, and mistakes to heal the void of her father.

Women such as myself were born to nurture, love, show affection, and to be loved. If those attributes aren't experienced in a woman's childhood, she will search for examples of those natural qualities for the rest of her life. When you are a child you believe and take in everything you see and feel from the people around you. You learn from your mother, father, and others whether a thing is wrong or right. Everything my father did was somewhat right to me, but deep down I knew some of it was wrong. I was able to figure out the wrong after he began to make me feel his absence in beginning a new life with the "other woman." I feel the spirit of jealousy, bitterness, and anger during my childhood increased from the heartbreak of my father. I felt jealousy because I didn't want my father to go and be with another woman and her kids. I believed it would only take all of his love and time from me. The bitterness crept in when I would think of him being with her each day instead of me. Anger was experienced when my father broke his promises to me even when he didn't think he promised me anything.

Fathers, the promise starts when you help create your daughter and the moment she is born. I always thought fathers should make a vow to their daughters as long as you both shall live.

Father to Daughter Vow

The vow to honor and cherish your daughter for the rest of her life. To have and to hold her from all hurt and danger. To be available through sickness and health. To love and cherish her all the days of her life.

This vow to your daughter should be more than solemn to you. It should be sacred as well. This is a vow to never break her heart just as you would never break your wife's heart. I'm sure my father made a vow to the "other woman," yet never made one to me as his daughter. If the vow was made between me and my dad I feel spiritually that it would have eliminated a lot of heartache and pain in my future. Instead what should have been a sacred vow became the heartbreak of a lifetime.

For a long time in my adult years, I didn't believe in marriage because I was never given the example of a marriage from my parents. Until this day I wonder if my father ever thought about me or my brother when he made his vows to the "other woman." I'm assuming the "other woman" didn't care because as a woman I would have simply asked before stating vows. "don't you want to include you children in this?" The question was never asked, however. The "other woman" was only thinking of herself and did what she had to do to get my Daddy. As I write this I don't even think she knew how my father's absence affected me. The "other woman" becomes accountable for destroying the lives of all children involved. I may have smiled and played during my times with my father and his woman, but deep down inside I was always in pain and confused. This type of emotion really impacted my life for days to come. I always felt as if my father betrayed me. I had not only lost my father being in my life. I had lost him to a woman I felt he put before me. I've suffered from depression throughout my life and always thought it came from things that happened in my adult life. My depression actually began in my childhood and I really didn't recognize what I was feeling. It was never dealt with. Insecurities were ignited as well during my childhood because I lost trust in my father. I lacked confidence because I couldn't figure out my worth. My father killed the idea of worth. Until this day I don't think my father realized the consequences of his actions and it was so hard to have those *Why?* conversations.

FOUR
THE DADDYLESS BEHAVIOR

Studies have shown that as women grow older, the impact of a father's absence or infidelity grows over time; increasing as those women grow up and try to form their own relationships. Daughters of absent fathers have less trust in men, lower expectations of their relationships and a lack of confidence. For me, these studies have proven true. I didn't realize that the older I got I would lose trust for people, have temporary relationships, and think that every man who smiled in my face was the one or could be the one.

During middle school and high school, I was very insecure with my weight and always thought no one would like me because I was "fat." During my preteen years, the boys were very harsh on the girls and I was bullied daily, however I had a defensive attitude. I would always fight back verbally and physically. I was never taught nor told life lessons on how to ignore people or not to care what people think. I never knew how a girl should be treated by a young man. A better way of life was not shown to me. The determination developing in me seemed so invisible to me as a child because clearly at that age I didn't know what determination was. I would act out at school, show aggressive behavior, and wore my feelings right on my shoulders. As I got older that became a somewhat positive aspect of my determination as I learned to curtail it, as a young girl, however it had a completely different effect on me and those I came into contact with. As a young girl, I deemed it negative determination because during that time I didn't know any better than to prove to people and things around me that I wasn't going to be messed with. I also determined that if my father was not in my life that was the way I would be for the rest of my life.

When I graduated high school I went off to college because I was determined to refute statistics of uneducated fatherless daughters. By the time I entered college, I was in pure denial that I was still searching for my father's love and position in life. At that point, I determined I was full grown and should have overcome the heartbreak and inconsistent involvement dealt to me by my father. I quickly confessed I was fooling myself.

I was a young country girl who moved to the city. I was a freshman in college and the boys there were very persuasive and handsome. I claimed I was only having fun when hanging around these boys, but with the ears of my heart I listened to what they would say hoping some notion would sound like my father and fill my void.

While in college I still held on to my high school sweetheart. He was still in high school with one year remaining. At the same time, I was dealing with a guy from my hometown as well. I was just lost when it came to loving a guy because I felt that every guy I ran with would love me and make me forget about my childhood. I soon learned those guys were after one thing only; my body and what I had between my legs. I didn't know any better. The only thing on my mind was to prove to my father that I was more than just a girl he could throw away. Throughout life I have said things such as this;

"Oh you didn't show up at my high school graduation, I'll show him. You didn't show up in my life, oh I'll show him."

Those words were forming my positive determination, but were also causing me to become vulnerable to so many men as I was in search of my father. I didn't know that those words were setting me up to become a determined woman. My love for my father was so strong that getting with another man would help me get over his absence. I even began dating an older man I met while in college. I was so lost from fatherlessness that I became lost in every relationship I entered with men. In 2002, I compromised my true identity as a woman. I entertained multiple men while trying to sustain my grades. I soon became pregnant with my first child (motivation). I decided I couldn't live with myself having my first child at 20 years old while in college. I just knew this child belonged to my high school sweetheart because he was the one I messed around with the most. He was the one I always thought reminded me so much of my father. By the time I became pregnant, my relationship with my high school sweetheart was over and done. I became so depressed with being pregnant, I believed it initiated the end of my life, but that good ole determination I had toward my father of "I'll show him" was still upon me. I soon came to my senses and declared I would have my baby, finish college and show my father I was somebody. Not once did my father ask me if I needed anything nor was he present during my first pregnancy and college years. As usual, my mother was busy keeping her and my brother's life afloat. I was basically on my own in college, but my mom did support me during my pregnancy. All the while my high school sweetheart was getting his plans squared away to enter college as well. I lived on campus while I was pregnant because I didn't really show during my pregnancy; however living in dorms while pregnant was a big violation. That ole' determination was kicking me in my butt even harder at this point because I was determined to expedite my path regardless of the fact I was with child. After I birthed my first child I went back home for a little while to get things together with myself, my child, and my child's father. Things began to become shaky because my high school sweetheart wanted a blood test to determine if my baby was his. I responded that would be fine because I was certain he was my child's father. During this time there was still no relationship nor attention from my father at all, so as soon as my maternity leave was over I packed up and went back to college because I had something to prove to him. My mom took care of my baby girl and let me go back to college. I just didn't want to sit down in my hometown and become another statistic. When I got back to college I decide to try it again, but at a much better college and atmosphere. I transferred to a university in the same city. Things were going great, but my heart was still in broken pieces. I was constantly fighting with my high school sweetheart and his new girlfriend, so I finally gave him that blood test he wanted. After a long dreadful wait the test results came back and I received a call from my mother while partying on the yard. I was still entertaining whoever smiled in my face and thought it felt good.

My mom told me directly, "he is not the father." Those five words caused me to fall instantly to my knees and go ballistic. I believe this was the start of my feeling like a failure in life. I couldn't believe it and the news put me in a state of shock. I cried until I couldn't cry anymore and all I could think was; "how could this be true?" I instantly remember that during college I had messed around with three other guys, but never more than my high school sweetheart. I just wanted love and not another heartbreak, but it led to my becoming a single mother very early.

With the help of my mother, I was able to gather myself and decided to test the three other guys I messed around with. When the test came back it was proven neither of them were the father of my child.

At this point I wanted to kill myself.

I was lost, hurt, shameful, and suicidal. In spite of this downfall, I was determined to be someone. I was also determined to find my child's father and not become a disgrace to society (at least that's how I felt at the time). My mother stated "I don't know what you've been doing, but you need to test every man you have been with in any way. I was so lost I couldn't think of any more men. You see, when I involved myself with those men, I felt pain and as a result I put them out of my mind and tried not to think of them if they didn't give the love I needed or filled the void left by my father. In order to find my child's father, I had to confront my past again.

With all of this happening my actions began to resemble the same behavior I would dish out when I wanted my father as a young girl. It soon dawned on me that there was one last man I was involved with, but doubted he was my child's father. I didn't think he was it because he didn't come close to penetrating me in a deep way. The majority of our time together was foreplay. I am referring to the older man I met and didn't really like. Well, I tested him and he was the father. I was heartbroken all over again because I knew this would ignite the cycle of fatherlessness in my daughter's life. This man was not at all husband material. I was just done. I was failing college and depressed, but determination didn't let me go. I continued fighting a battle with my child's father because I knew we weren't going to be together. He retaliated and would not support her because of that. I had to move on with my life. I placed him on child support, and made him a thing of the past. If I wanted to be a woman of integrity and value I could not put myself in that type of situation again. Once again, I was looking for love in many wrong places. I was determined to never place me or my child in that type of situation again. I had to be an example for my daughter as well. Life was teaching me some hard lessons but I was determined to continue to past the test and not let my past continue to test me.

I had become a fatherless daughter, college student, worker, and single mom. My determination sparked absence from my child's life because she was living with my mom and I was determined to still finish college. In college I felt alone and lost. Even though I was determined to prove to my father he missed out on having a relationship with me, all I have ever wanted throughout my life was love, love, and more love. Through the years my life became more immersed in working, clubbing, trying to finish my bachelor's degree, and keeping a roof over my head. Remember, the atmosphere of adulthood began for me when I was a small child, therefore when I became independent, it wasn't hard to be an adult, but it was hard for me to maintain bills and school. My promiscuous behavior throughout college cried out for my father's love.

Research determines single mothers will date several men to find a suitable mate for her and her children. More often than not, the female child she bares will learn dating behavior very early by mimicking her mother. This is very true because I began dating and seeking love in that manner. By this time my emotions and thoughts of life and fatherlessness were all over the place, so I would look for someone who would be a bandage for my emotions and hurt. I know the emotional hurt from my father and wounds from life events manifested my promiscuous behavior. When it occurred, I didn't think the inconsistency of my father would show my desperation and need for attention from a male. I constantly met men who were ready to give the attention I was so desperately needing. I really thought the men I met wanted to give me that love the right way, but many of those men wanted to add to my hurt and emotions. I soon met this guy whom I believed would be the one. He was tall, light skinned, had beautiful eyes and was very charming. He was new to the area (which I thought was a plus). Considering all I'd been through I felt I couldn't find a good man because I was a single mother already. From witnessing my mother's life and the lives of other women, I felt a woman could not find a good man if she already had children, however I wouldn't allow my single-mom status to determine my future love life and potential. I really didn't get to know this guy because as long as he was showing me love I really didn't need to know anything else. How crazy was that? I would always ask him about his life and family, but he would always respond that all of his family was dead. He also stated he had several children. I should have listened to those words and taken heed, but I kept going and thought it would be perfect for me and my daughter to be become his family one day. After "dating" this guy for a couple months, he would let me come over to his place, but we never went to dinner or anything. I really didn't know how a man was supposed to date a woman. I was only concerned with whether or not he showed me love. This relationship with this man became sexual only.

I ended up with another darkness in my life.

I became pregnant in 2004 with my second child (motivation). After finding out, I became distraught. Whenever I would have sex with this man he would tell me, "I'm not taking care of any more kids." I would always think he was just saying that. The day came when I would find out I was with child yet again and after rushing out of the doctor's office, I immediately called him. He forcefully stated, "I don't care if you are having a snake, I don't want no more kids!" I will never forget those words because the thought of having another child without their father felt like death to me. I sat in the car and cried my eyes out. Not only did I feel I let my mother down again, I completely felt I totally let myself down. It seemed like crying became a daily routine for me. I would always hear my mother's voice saying, "Carlisa you are always crying." Well that was basically my life; full of tears, hurt, and abuse. My behavior was really speaking for my life. I was lost and confused with so many unanswered questions. At this point, my girls had two different fathers and I became more shameful of my life. I made up my mind that I was not going to have another child without a committed father to care for them. One day I decided to call my mother and tell her I was going to abort my second child because I couldn't bare taking care of another child alone. My mother became very upset declaring what God would do to me if I did that, but I honestly didn't care. I had lost all hope for most everything in my life, but realized one thing remained--my determination. I knew that abortion would not be a good choice, but I was determined I wouldn't become another "single-mom" statistic. After the argument with my mother, I hung up the phone and went straight to the clinic. I sat in my car for about an hour asking God to forgive me for what I was about to do. As I read the name of the clinic I was certain this was the right place to get an abortion. At this clinic I was given options on my unplanned pregnancy, yet at the same time after going inside, watching their videos, taking another pregnancy test, etc., it seemed their aim was more in the direction of persuading me to change my mind. As the ultrasound began, I saw my child's heartbeat even though she was only the shape and size of a peanut. I instantly became emotional and couldn't visualize having an abortion. I felt as though aborting my child would be murder. Being the Christian I am, I would never be able to live with myself knowing I did something of this magnitude. Needless to say, I changed my mind.

After I left the clinic, the crying, stressing, and hurt continued to haunt my life. I thought about my father every single day. I wanted to be in his arms again hearing him sing. That is the only thing that would have made me feel safe and alright. The hate from my childhood continued for the days to come. A few months passed and I was around 7 months pregnant, still in college, working, toggling single-motherhood, fighting for my second child's father to get involved in her life, and dealing with my own demons. With such a heavy load on my shoulders and major pregnancy complications, I went into early labor. At this time, I really didn't have many friends, but lived about an hour away from my mom and family.

While cleaning one day, my water broke and I rushed myself to the ER. There were no contractions so I remained hospitalized for a week while doctors worked to prevent a premature birth. Toward the end of that week I went into labor with no one by my side. My mom was still a work-a-holic and she wasn't able to be there. After giving birth to a beautiful baby girl, I was ready to leave the hospital and get my life back on track, but I didn't know I had a long road ahead of me. My second child was kept in NICU due to her premature birth, so between school and work I would visit her every day. One day I decided to go visit her father and tell him I had the baby, but when I got to him he didn't want anything to do with me anymore. I was both hurt and angry and wondered why he didn't want to deal with me or his child. As most immature men do, he began claiming the child wasn't his, however I proved very quickly that she was.

After my daughter was well enough to go home, I sent her to live with my mother and stepfather and took her father to child support court. As a child and young adult I couldn't embrace the happiness of my youth because my behavior and actions placed me in stress that was beyond my years. As a young adult I felt I should have been enjoying life single, free and happy. Life, however, was not setup that way for me and I blamed my father so much for most of it. Very often I think that if my father had been active in my life it would have turned out so differently. With both parents involved and in love with their child, I truly believe I would have made better choices. I knew life had to get better for me. I still was determined to prove to my father and everyone else that I wasn't going to allow the odds against me to stop the plan God had for my life. I continued my journey as a single mom aiming to maintain my life the best way I knew how. I received no phone calls whatsoever from my own father when I got pregnant and had my daughters. I always wondered the person who helped make me could go from being the love of my life to a total stranger. I really became used to fatherlessness. The behaviors of my childhood spilled over into my adult life and I ended up paying great consequences for my behavior. Maintaining determination and staying focused became a great battle in my life and most times giving up was winning. In spite of the opposition, something deep down just wouldn't let me give in and become a statistic in society. I was now the mother of two beautiful daughters who became my motivation and added fuel to my determination.

The cycle of fatherlessness continued on in me and was inherited by my daughters lives as well. I pretty much felt as though. I was cursed (doomed) for the rest of my life, however there was one thing I knew for sure; determination and doom did not have anything in common and as long as I kept determination I could break the cycle somehow.

FIVE
THE DADDYLESS CYCLE

It is said that a family cycle can be an unconscious repetition that will continue throughout a family until an adult relieves the cycle. A dysfunctional behavioral problem usually begins early on in a family bloodline. After the cycle began in my mother's upbringing with unstable living arrangements, it continued and became prevalent all the way down to my daughters. After growing weary of the life I lived in Alabama, I decided to choose another path for myself and my daughters. I knew this new life would not meet my mother's approval, but I believed my life would be embraced and attract the love I needed if I made the change I'd decided on. I experienced a great deal of change during my time in Alabama and began dating women. I had given up on men and determined I was this way from childhood. Some believe I became gay because of molestation or due to my father's absence, however for me the feeling was much deeper. I knew I was happy and finally felt genuine deep love with a woman for the first time in my life.

College graduation arrived and with so many long hard days and nights of studying and hard work, I finally graduated with my bachelor's degree. I was indeed proud of myself yet still very unhappy with my life deep down. My life had taken a complete 360 degree turn and I had two babies I was responsible for. My father didn't show up at my graduation and for me, that was fine. I came to accept his absence after seeing it time and time again. I finally accepted the fact my dad had missed out on so much in my life and disappeared when I needed him most, therefore it made no sense to me that I should expect his presence at my graduation.

While dating women and hanging around friends who were engaged in the lesbian lifestyle with me I felt love and comfort like never before and didn't want to change. Each day I questioned if it was right for me and my daughters, but my happiness had taken priority by that time. After so many failed dating episodes in my life I was just over men. When I was with men I didn't feel anything at all. I felt loving another woman was right for me. I began to date a woman out of town and we immediately connected. After graduating I decided to move to Atlanta with her and my daughters. I longed for a family and even though we didn't reflect a traditional family, I was determined to live above statistics. Again, I was making daddyless decisions.

Both my daughter's fathers were absent from their lives. I gave up on efforts to involve them and I was equally tired of making the effort to involve my own dad in my life. I felt as though moving to a different state would give me a new lease on life. I just wanted to get away from it all, however I honestly believed I was repeating the same cycle as my mom did when she plucked up my brother and I and moved us to another state.

After living with my ex-partner for several months our relationship had become toxic. There was a great deal of arguing and fighting happening around my daughters. I knew that was not the life I wanted for them so I left and sent my daughters to live with my mother in Alabama. Doing that was a tough decision, but I knew I couldn't make it in a big city with two children. I was determined to stay away from Alabama and moving backwards was not an option for me. I wanted to move forward and not become another statistic. In life you are either going to beat the system or let the system beat you. I set in place my own system and plan for survival.

I found myself alone in Atlanta afraid of failing again from past mistakes. Trusting in people to be my hope of love, security and comfort was not working. I never looked for anyone to support me and I remained independent, however that in itself brought on a lot of debt. The thoughts kept coming in regards to my father. He never once helped me and gave excuses as to why he couldn't. He would always bring up this one computer he bought me while in school that I didn't keep payments on. It ended up on his credit and he never forgot about that. After hearing him replay that incident over and over again, I totally stopped asking my father for anything. My mother was not financially stable enough to help me either but she took my daughters back and that was the biggest help she could have ever done. I will be forever grateful for that.

Momma…
you may not have been the best
But you helped me every
day to stand the test.
Even though daddy made me
I clearly know

Carlisa Johnson

That Momma raised me
Daddy failed, but Momma
You helped me prevail

Those were some of the words that kept me going while living alone in Atlanta. In the back of my mind I would always say, "I don't want to go through the cycle my mother went through with my brother and I don't want to be a single mom like my mom was." The cycle still continued with me, however. The voice of God would always whisper that the cycle would stop with me and I was the one who would birth a new thing in my bloodline. I was determined to let that happen but the past would continue to haunt me. I went through many court battles with my first child's father for child support and my second daughter's father was nowhere to be found. I found the paternal side of my daughter's family on social media and reached out to them. After I found an older half–sister of hers we connected for a while. After she asked her father about my daughter he immediately denied she was his daughter. I was angry and hurt all over again. I thought that after years had passed, he would have come to his senses, but he didn't. I also reached out to one of his sister's via social media as well as his father's side--still no luck. I was determined to make sure my daughters each had a relationship with their fathers. At the same time I remembered, no one can make a man do anything he doesn't want to and I instantly gave up. I came to the reality that fatherless for my daughters and I would be a part of my life. The question I kept pondering was, Why doesn't a man want to be in his child's life? I knew I had to stop this vicious cycle, but didn't know how. Many believe we develop from the world around us and move the trends of life, but we are more often a product of our upbringing. As we age, our immediate world either teaches us we can become more or less than what we came from. I chose to be more. I wanted more out of life, more for my daughters, and more for generations to come after us.

My daughters continued living with my mother, but I knew I would soon have to get them and raise them myself though I was still severely unprepared. I was not ready to be a full-time single mom. Even after failed relationships I still continued to date and look for love. While going through these changes there were some positive constants that existed in my life. I had great church home, supportive friends, and felt loved. Church and singing in the choir were my safe haven. I realized I just needed love and support. I was only in my late 20's and been through more than the average 40-year-old. I was exhausted from life. I was missing my daughters, desiring to establish a relationship with my father, and wanted my daughters to do the same with their fathers as well. Every year I would determine, "I'm going to move my daughters back in with me," but I'll have to make sure it's the right time and I will need to be certain I am settled. In the back of my mind I knew the time would never be right. Considering my financial situation, my daughters would be adults by the time I got my life together. I thought about their education as well. The schools in my hometown had become worse than when I was their age. I knew I wanted to afford them the best education possible. That was a thought that continued to linger in my mind.

As I continued to date, I met women who didn't want to date another woman with children. I found myself in one relationship that I thought was perfect until the woman stated she didn't want to be a step mom. Before I fell in love with her I told her I had children, but she didn't care. I was devastated. One night I ended up in jail as a result of fighting with one of my ex-partners for the first time. I saw my life flash before my eyes after being in jail with women I clearly didn't relate to. While in there I ministered to and counseled some of those women and immediately realized imprisonment was not for me. Enough was enough. I was bailed out the next day by my mother and my ex was still trying to stay and remain toxic in my life. Regardless of all we had been through up until then, I ended up taking her back. I realized I would forget what she did, but I would never forgive. Forgiveness is a hard thing, but I know it's something I will have to do for a lot of people who have caused harm in my life.

After another fight, I looked myself in the mirror and said, "I cannot continue like this". This wasn't a moment I felt I should go back to men because it wasn't about who I was dating. It was about what I needed to change in me. God gave me chance after chance and even cleared my name from the charge that sent me to jail. I realized after the toxic relationships ended it was time to heal and reinvent myself. I decided to take a break from church and life ended up very lonely again.

Daddy...

You question me about being gay
But you never questioned me about my day
Not one "How was your day?" or "How was your night?"
I'm at a point to show you that
I will succeed without you with all my might!

Those thoughts became my motivation and motto for life. Even if he didn't see or ask about my accomplishments I knew one day he would notice. I became hard on myself when I failed and questioned my self-worth. I also got to a point where I felt my life was settling without my daughters in it. I felt I was being punished by God and that if my daughters were in my care life would have been so much better.

I ended up going back to my church home where I believed I'd met the woman who would become the love of my life. The charm was different, the affection was different and the love was different. I thought, she has to be the one. In the beginning we experienced shaky ground, but she would always try to make things right. After sharing the yearning I had for my children to be with me, she immediately said, "let's go get your girls and be a family." At first I was shocked and didn't believe her, but when she began to look for a bigger place for us I was in complete awe. In the in the back of my mind I thought, is it finally my time to have someone help me raise my kids? I was the main bread-winner in our relationship and she was very young, but smart with two degrees. I felt she would eventually get a good job. I informed my mother I was going to finally move the girls in with me, but my mom and daughters were sad about the decision. My daughters didn't want to be away from my mom, but I had to do what I needed to do for all of us. I now had my partner, a new house, and my girls. I believed I was finally living the life. Things were a little rough at first with my daughters trying to adjust to a new state and school. They were so behind in school that learning became difficult for them. Beating the odds became easy for me, however, so I kept the faith and pushed them and myself.

Shortly after we were settled, my health began to plummet. I developed a weight-related illness and a nerve disease. I had quite a few questions for the man upstairs. I wondered why my life had taken yet another drastic turn. I had my girls and believed life could only get better, but it got worse first. The nerve disease in my face became worse and the pain grew to an unbearable level. This disease was also called Trigeminal Neuralgia "suicide disease" because the pain was just that bad. As the pain became intensified I became less patient and angrier. Some days my partner had to take care of everything for me and my daughters because I just couldn't. Her patience soon began to wear out, however I tried to keep our relationship afloat through the pain. I worked a job where I had to talk all the time while in pain. I failed to spend time with my daughters and I often rested immediately after coming home from work because I had no energy to give anyone else. The meds were not working and all the doctors were doing was increasing my dose. As the dosage increased my energy and motivation decreased. My nerve pain continued to fluctuate so I had to have several surgeries. By this time, me and my partner were drifting apart. She had no more patience to deal with me and my illness nor my daughters.

After a year of living together I discovered she was unfaithful, however I still tried to stay the course with her. Amid the cheating, fussing and fighting I realized I'd placed my daughters in yet another toxic situation. My ex begged to stay in my life after the cheating and I believed that if someone wanted to remain in my life that was a good sign because I'd had so many to give up on me in the past. I gave her another chance.

Soon after re-establishing the relationship with my girlfriend, I found myself researching the name of my second daughters father. His name appeared beneath one search in connection with a murder case. I couldn't believe what I was seeing so I continued to research more and found more. My youngest daughter's father murdered his first wife 16 years prior to my discovery of his article. Before her demise, she had suddenly gone missing for two years. After he murdered her he buried her in the woods and her body was discovered years later. A television show called Cold Justice Case on TNT came to the home of my youngest child's father and randomly pulled cold case files. They happened to pull my youngest child's father case. Upon learning all of this I screamed to the top of my lungs! I told my girlfriend that my daughter's father was in jail for murdering his first wife. She immediately embraced me as I burst into tears. When I met her father he was actually on the run. I had been in pursuit of him all this time and had no idea he was a murder. He could have done the same to me as he'd done with his ex. I sat and watch the video of this murder case a thousand times and discovered a lot about him that I was in the dark about. There were also other victims. All of the men and women interviewed reduced me to tears because I could have been

a victim as well. I thanked God he prevented me from continuing in a relationship with this man, yet sad my daughter would have to live fatherless for the remainder of her life.

So there I was needing love, attention, and support I didn't get as a child. How could I give something to my daughters that I didn't have. My relationship with my girlfriend became very toxic. After two years of living together she decided she didn't want the relationship with me anymore. I fought to keep her because I felt she was the only person who took the time to love me and give me what I needed. After one last fight with her and her family, she put me and my daughters out of her house. I couldn't believe this was happening to me. I began thinking about all of my life disappointments and once again I was ready to send my daughters back with my mother. I was beginning to give up, but I was quickly reminded of the curse I was chosen to break in my bloodline. God sent me a revelation of who I was and who I was to become. I never labeled myself a lesbian. I embraced who I loved and who loved me and women were the ones who actually loved me. My longest and deepest relationships were with women. For a while I hated both of my partners for what they did to me and my daughters by putting us in unstable situations, but I realized I played an important role in those toxic relationships as well. I knew I couldn't hold my partners responsible for anything outside of their own actions.

I look at me and I looked at my daughters and immediately activated my determination not to allow anyone to devalue my worth anymore. By this time in my life I knew God had a plan for me and because I had been through so much. Upon that realization, I began to value and love myself more. I realized that love had to begin with me. I also knew I had a long road ahead of me.

#DaddylessDetermination Checklist:

- ✓ Forgive Him
- ✓ Forgive Yourself
- ✓ Never Give Up
- ✓ Keep Moving Forward
- ✓ Eliminate Daddyless Excuses
- ✓ Think Positive
- ✓ Trust the Plan of God
- ✓ Stay DETERMINE

SIX
THE DADDYLESS REVELATION

Revelation is God's way of showing his will and supplying human knowledge of divine things to come. As I sat in my small two-bedroom house with my daughters, I realized after all I'd been through it was time to make a change. I felt alone, but God was gearing my vision towards him and what he wanted me to do. Writing this book is one of them. After the break up with my last girlfriend, my first priority was to find a way to become pain free from my nerve disease. I schedule my final surgery. This surgery would be a major one-- brain surgery. I was so afraid, alone, and angry with life. My mother came and was willing to help me with my daughters while I recovered from my surgery.

During the time of my brain surgery scheduling, I worked for an insurance company. I was promoted while there and had to attend a 9-week training class. Within those weeks, I had to figure out how I would squeeze in the surgery. I didn't want to take up the new position with the severe pain I was experiencing. I was also still finishing up my Master's Degree in Public Health. I was dealing with a lot emotionally and still pressing on to finish another degree, toggle the loss of a bad relationship, two daughters, and a nerve disease.

I was determined.

Soon after finishing up two interviews the employer I had been interviewing for decided to hire someone else. I took that decision with a grain of salt and quickly let it go. I continued my training and soon after, my job let me go on leave to have my brain surgery. I would have to work extra hard to get caught up with my training when I returned.

After surgery, my doctors told my mom the surgery was very challenging. I recovered, nonetheless with the hands and protection of God and my mother and daughters by my side. After my quick recovery, I went back to training for my job and began to get my life back on track. I was looking forward to being pain free again. Within a week, post-surgery I got a call from the same company about the same position I didn't get. The recruiter stated that the person they hired was not qualified for the position and immediately asked me if I wanted it. I was excited and nervous at the same time. I was in disbelief. I told the recruiter to give me a couple days to think about it because I would start on a one-year contract with the potential of becoming permanent.

With this pending decision, I was stuck in between staying at my permanent job and transitioning to a contract position in my career field. I immediately prayed and got advice from friends before making the decision to step out on faith. I couldn't believe after recuperating from brain surgery that I had the same job I wanted still waiting on me. I knew God was up to something and I was ready to follow His lead. I took the position and upon beginning, my supervisor stated that this job was for me. The following month I graduated with my Master's Degree in Public Health. I shed tears of joy thanking God for continuing to shield me from harm as He had done my entire life. After setting aside my obstacles, I became pain free, finished school, and   permanent at my job as well. Look at God! Through all I'd been through I became a professional, philanthropist, author, and professional MUA all because I became a DETERMINED woman armed with the experiences of my past.

Once again, I didn't hear from my father at all. My surgery was successful and I went back to work within three weeks. Yes, I recovered from brain surgery in three weeks! That's when I discovered God was up to something in my life.

One day while riding home from work I began to think about my father very heavily. He was the one person I thought of the most. I wondered if he even knew all my life had succumbed to. God whisper to me, "the only way to let him know is to tell your story."

Here I am today telling my story.

I realize my thoughts were leading me
to who God called me to be,
The thoughts were for my good.
The daddyless thoughts evolved me,
The thoughts were for my good.
Through trials and tribulation that I endured,
The thoughts were for my Good.

Many would say my current lifestyle loving the same sex is because of my daddyless thoughts, lack of love, or all I went through. That is not the case. I came to realize this lifestyle depicted who I really was. I dealt with men because I was looking for my father in all of them, however I had no real interest in any of them. Many may not agree with what I'm saying and that's ok. That is another book and story I will tell later. I am free, my family loves me, and as for my father we really don't communicate much or discuss my lifestyle. The revelation of my daddyless thoughts reminded me that God established all things through his word and reveals the confirmation of himself through our realities. Those constant thoughts made me push through my realities of self-love, struggles, and adversity. Through all of the abuse, neglect, rejection, and struggles I endured one would think I should be dead by now, but I'm yet alive. Determination was the driving force of my life and I still feel to this day that God and determination kept me alive. I learned I invited things into my life through thoughts. Affirming positive thoughts will end in a positive life and affirming negative thoughts will do the opposite. As I thought about my father, I dwelled on how I could be different than him. I began affirming my life every day. I had to become a motivation for my daughters as well. I began turning my story into success. I knew ever since I was a little girl that the power of my life was determined through God and my way of thinking. My father was not a bad person, he actually is a great guy, but as I said previously a person cannot give you what they don't have. I don't blame my father for everything that happened in my life. My heavenly father kept me through all the struggles I had to go through to become that determined woman. I realized all of the tears I shed throughout those years of wanting my father in my life became the water to my seed that allowed me to grow. Sometimes my thoughts were not good, but when I applied determination to my thoughts they became good.

God chose my dad to be my father.

Today, I live my life freely and on purpose. Determination made me realize who I was and who I will become. Determination became my love. Stay tuned…..

Carlisa Johnson

My Earthly Father Made Me, But My Heavenly Father Kept Me

You were my dad that I once knew
But little do you know the pain you put me through
I've grown up and realized
I had the drive
To always stay strong and alive
I'm your daughter
And you're my father
Do you ever have thoughts of me too?
As I look at my life through my thoughts
I know that Daddy made but
Momma raised me
Through all of my struggles
My earthly father was distance
But my Heavenly father was always persistent
The good book always says to forgive
But I'm still trying to forget
In reality I don't blame you for the lack of
I just wish you would had risen above

Daddy, I'm the only woman who thinks of you

To All Daddyless Daughters

From My Daughters and I

Photo/Book Cover Credit: Ralph Edward

www.ingramcontent.com/pod-product-compliance
Lightning Source LLC
Chambersburg PA
CBHW062121080426
42734CB00012B/2938